Noisytime for Zoo Animals

by Caroline Arnold   **photographs by Richard Hewett**

Carolrhoda Books, Inc./Minneapolis

A zoo can be a noisy place. What kinds of sounds do zoo animals make?

ostrich

A lion roars.

lion

A cheetah snarls.

cheetah

Elephants rumble.

elephants

 sea lion barks.

sea lion

A peacock screams.

peacock

A young hippopotamus squeals.

hippopotamus

A penguin honks.

penguins

Parrots squawk.

parrots

 bobcat hisses.

bobcat

A giraffe snorts.

giraffe

An elk bellows.

elk

A monkey chatters.

monkey

Each animal talks in its
very own way.
"Hello," "watch out," and
"go away" are some things
their noises mean.
What kinds of things
do you like to say?

camels

Where can I find...

polar bear

Caroline Arnold has written more than one hundred books for children. Many of the books are about animals. Caroline lives with her husband in Los Angeles, California.

Richard Hewett worked for magazines before he discovered children's books. He, too, has created many books about animals. Richard lives with his wife in Los Angeles, California.

Text copyright © 1999 by Caroline Arnold
Photographs copyright © 1999 by Richard R. Hewett
Additional photograph courtesy of: © Caroline Arnold, page 31

This book is available in two bindings:
ISBN 1-57505-289-X (lib. bdg.)
ISBN 1-57505-392-6 (trade bdg.)

Carolrhoda Books, Inc., c/o The Lerner Publishing Group
241 First Avenue North, Minneapolis, MN 55401 U.S.A.

Website address: www.lernerbooks.com

Library of Congress Cataloging-in-Publication Data

Arnold, Caroline.
    Noisytime for zoo animals / by Caroline Arnold ; photographs by Richard Hewett.
        p.   cm.
    Includes index.
    Summary: In photographs and simple text, describes the wide variety of sounds made by animals in the zoo.
    ISBN 1-57505-289-X (lib. bdg.: alk. paper)
    1. Zoo animals—Vocalization—Juvenile literature. 2. Animal sounds—Juvenile literature. [1. Zoo animals. 2. Animal sounds.] I. Hewett, Richard, ill. II. Title.
QL77.5.A83 1999
636.088'9—dc21   98-24376

Manufactured in the United States of America
1 2 3 4 5 6 – JR – 04 03 02 01 00 99